# TRUE CASES OF A PRIVATE INVESTIGATOR

Marshall Cavendish
Editions

Cover design by Cover Kitchen Ltd
Book design by Benson Tan
Text by Yeo Suan Futt & Heng Ping Kai



Published by Marshall Cavendish Editions
An imprint of Marshall Cavendish International
Times Centre, 1 New Industrial Road, Singapore 536196
Tel: (65) 6213 9300 Fax: (65) 6285 4871
E-mail: genref@sg.marshallcavendish.com
Online Bookstore: www.marshallcavendish.com/genref

Other Marshall Cavendish offices
Marshall Cavendish Ltd. PO Box 65829, London EC1P 1NY, UK • Marshall Cavendish Corporation. 99 White Plains Road, Tarrytown NY 10591-9001, USA • Marshall Cavendish International (Thailand) Co Ltd. 253 Asoke, 12th Flr, Sukhumvit 21 Road, Klongtoey Nua, Wattana, Bangkok 10110, Thailand • Marshall Cavendish (Malaysia) Sdn Bhd, Times Subang, Lot 46, Subang Hi-Tech Industrial Park, Batu Tiga, 40000 Shah Alam, Selangor Darul Ehsan, Malaysia



National Library Board, Singapore Cataloguing-in-Publication Data
Heng, Ping Kai.
True cases of a private investigator / Heng Ping Kai. – Singapore : Marshall Cavendish Editions, c2012.
p. cm.
ISBN : 978-981-4361-19-4 (pbk.)
1. Investigations. 2. Private investigators – Singapore. I. Title.
HV8099
363.289095957 -- dc23 OCN782999887

Printed in Singapore by Times Printers Pte Ltd

# CONTENTS

# NOTE

The contents of the following pages are all based on true cases from the private investigator's files. However, all names and other identifying features have been changed to protect the innocent and not so innocent.

# CHAPTER 1

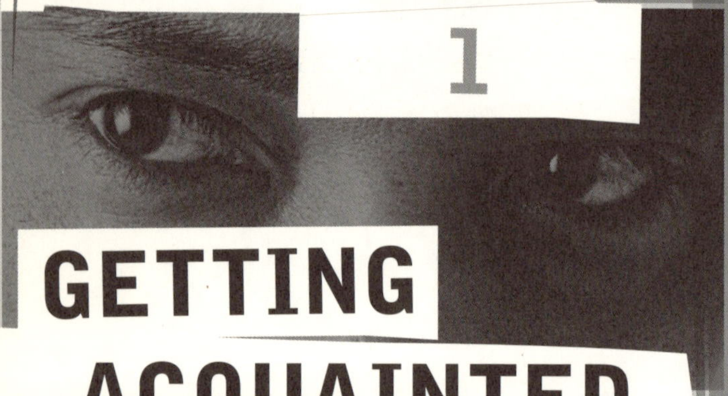

# GETTING ACQUAINTED

We've seen it a million times on television – guessing the murderer before the episode ends can be a national pastime especially if the cop drama is popular enough. However, the real life of a detective is not quite how it's often portrayed, and that of a private investigator is even hazier.

I do not mean to boast, but working largely without a firearm (a gun), a warrant, and especially not the whole authority of the state behind us, a private investigator (PI or private eye) is not very different from a hunter who lives off the land on what he can catch and kill – we live on our wits.

What I mean is, when it comes to the crunch, you can't even insult a police officer and get away with it, much less punch him in the face. But us private eyes, with no small amount of irony I might add, are all out in the open. It is not an unfair statement to say that the only means of protection between us and a broken tooth (or much worse) is an intangible veil of deception and confusion that we weave with tricks of the trade. Just so you know, this comes from experience, exceptional situational awareness honed by good training and pure dumb luck – in order of increasing importance.

This is not meant to ignore or downplay the Singapore Police Force (SPF), of course. If it weren't for the SPF, I and many like me wouldn't be where we are today, so thanks are due to the SPF for the training it gave me. And thinking back, I should have been able to make something of a career in the SPF, having joined practically in my teens. Heck, to the best of my knowledge, I was even the youngest to make investigator in the force. But bureaucracy is something too clumsy for my taste. While I'd be the first to admit there is immense empowerment from walking around with a badge – a warrant card is not just a laminated piece of paper, it bears the authority of the whole nation state behind it – bureaucracy all but renders this meaningless for me. Too limiting, it's just not my style to live from day to day, completing reports or filling in one form after another. This is the side you'll never see on *Crime Watch* or even *Hawaii-Five-O*. It's just not glamorous, or exciting. But paperwork is pretty much what a police officer does most of the time.

We can't just have the police running all over the place doing whatever each officer felt ought to be done in a random, uncoordinated fashion. There would be chaos. So there's the need for paperwork just to keep the SPF humming along as a single organisation. Whether it's reporting on daily operations, staff reports, down to the amount of stationery you are going to need for the next quarter, there's a proper piece of paper where it's got to be filled. Order. And madness. So I left. It boils down to temperament.

Other than this, a successful private investigator relies on many of the same skills and qualities that make a fine police officer. I am not referring to the role-model bits like honesty and a TV hero readiness to shed blood for justice – but hard-nosed surveillance and detective skills that have been employed to solve crime. Skills such as how to obtain information as desired by our clients, whether it's about a likely cheating spouse, or business partner who has been less than honest.

These days, people just can't be trusted, which is where we private eyes come in. We investigate everything from a spouse having afternoon delights on the side; a business partner who's been acting strange, and matchmaking prospects who've been less than honest.

The truth is often murky, it's a fruit on a high branch; and if you need someone a little cleverer, a little less shy and way more motivated than you to make a grab for it, give people like me a call. We can't guarantee that the truth is sweet – it can be bitter, and often, very sour – but those who still believe ignorance is bliss probably also believe one can wish upon a star, for real.

In my world, which I believe is the real world, information is power. The power to act; and if nothing more, the power of proper resolution, that people need to move on with their lives. Even if they are bruised, at least the bleeding has stopped, so to speak.

Think of us as the opposite of the psychiatrist. You pay a shrink lots of money to learn about yourself whereas you pay us to find out about the people and matters around you. When Google and speculation just won't do, but actual legwork is needed out in the real world.

How does one choose the right investigator? I think it's like picking your personal tailor. Price is important, but that's easier to negotiate and adapt than finding an investigator with the right combination of suitable mindset, skills, qualities and motivation. By the latter, I don't just mean the money you're going to pay him, it has to be more than that. For anything beyond the most basic cases, you have to see if, beyond a good track record, whether the private investigator you're going to hire shares the same vibes as you. This is the little bit of detective work you must take on for yourself, you have to see if the investigator has any interest in your case, beyond the matter of the fee, and it's something you'll be able to feel from his (or her) body language – if it's clear enough. Otherwise, chances are, you should just move down the list and find another.

Here, I won't launch into an all-singing, all-dancing self-praising ad, but I don't do too badly. At a little taller than 1.6 metres, with average physique, I'm your everyman; it's not difficult for me to melt into a crowd and observe anyone I need to. I look like a younger Jet Li – who looks very ordinary too, wouldn't you say? With strong eyebrows that can give a sense of fun yet scrunched into a frown to intimidate, and my ever readiness to slap on a wig, I dare say I'm quite the chameleon. This has enabled me to slip in and out of a crowd without drawing any more attention than I deem appropriate, while observing my quarry and taking notes in my head. That's ability, written in a pretty healthy track record. But the latter alone doesn't say everything. A "track record" by its nature is overly skewed towards successes; it doesn't say much about the reasons and circumstances where we did not manage to get a good result. What is good? A result that is "conclusive" is not bad at all. Not every husband we've been tasked to tail is actually cheating on his wife, so if we can show that it is either of one eventuality with enough certainty, then that is a good result.

And another thing: some private investigators take Inspector Gadget as their role model. They've got mics and cameras coming out of their ears, in every size and configuration. It's a cool idea, but I personally do not believe in removing the intelligent operator from intelligence gathering. Call it old-fashioned if you will, but the spirit of a private investigator is his dogged determination, resourcefulness, and intelligence in reading people, situations, and responding in the most appropriate way to get the job done. And while the physical environment and situation may be dynamic enough, even more fluid is the human dynamic. You need people skills to befriend, to convince, even to intimidate, to gather all kinds of information which you will need to link together to produce something that is coherent, that is intelligible. You can't pick all that from a textbook or even simulated training scenarios; but one learns fast from getting punched in the face.

CHAPTER 2

# CHASING A TAIL

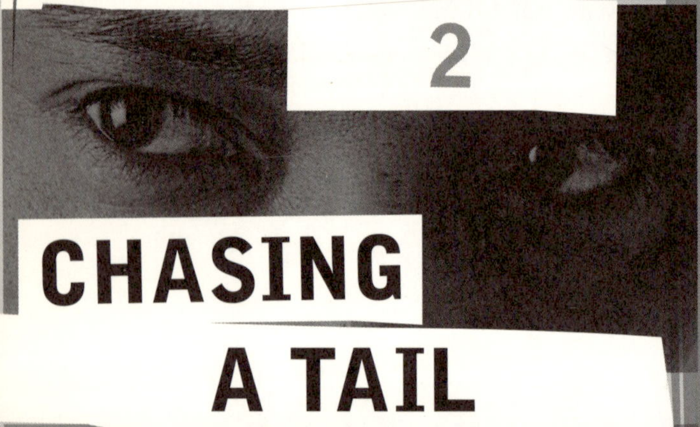

Mr Tan is no celebrity, just your average white collar worker. He was an operations manager and one can hardly get more colourless that. However when he left for work at 6:30 am one morning, with the sky above him barely lightening into another grey morning, three pairs of eyes were trained on him, without his knowledge.

Sitting in the car with me was Alice, my assistant. She is nothing much to look at beneath the frumpy floral dress, as she was meant to. I am dressed just as plainly, with a wig I picked myself. When I work, I always wear a wig. It's just part of the uniform and a handy mental switch to flit between work and personal time. Wear one as often as I do, and you'll understand why I shave my head clean, to take on multiple disguises in a flash. Together, Alice and I are as bland a couple as can be; no one would give us a second glance, which is how we like it when tailing someone.

About 20 metres ahead of us, leaning against the lamp post, and doing an admirable job of merging into the background is Chandran, dark as the paint on the post, and almost as thin. He appears to be reading the day's free tabloid, but he's really eyeballing our quarry.

Of course, we're not all going to shadow Mr Tan; it's Chandran for today. It's just important (and not to mention, professional) for the investigators on the case to have seen the subject rather than rely on photographs. In this particular case, Mr Tan looks to have aged, from the photo supplied by his wife. Middleaged, thinning hair, spectacles, slim built, in a white shirt (what else?) and work pants. There must be hundreds of men fitting such a description.

Chandran signalled to us and proceeded to shadow Mr Tan. Alice and I drove off to have breakfast.

The previous day...

"I suspect my husband is having an affair," Mrs Tan didn't mince her words. And she did not have the time to run after a hunch, that her husband was being unfaithful. This is where we come in. Normally I prefer to see my clients at our office, but this was a friend's friend, so to speak, and sometimes we go out of our way, even for these routine and "smaller" cases – those of a personal, rather than corporate nature. And I was curious. And where would an investigator be without curiosity?

She gave up her career as an accountant a few years ago to take care of her two young children. She had been occupied with housework since the family did not employ a maid. And from the photos displayed on the piano in her house, my prospective client seemed to have let herself go a little. Like many housewives on this well-trodden path, her transition from career woman to full-time housewife had brought with it a measure of insecurities, a shrinking of one's social circle; and with the latter, a little more weight, a little less powder on the face: predictably, she had become dowdy.

"What makes you say so?" I have lost count of the number of such cases I have encountered. I don't know if it's life in Singapore that's putting all this strain on marriages, or it's just us as people. If I had children, I wonder if I could tell them that I'm putting a roof over their heads and sending them to university on the back of anxieties around marriage; and I wonder a little what they'd say to that. We don't only do adultery cases, but checking on spouses could very well be the burger on the menu: the entre, and snooping about every thing else is a side dish.

"He's always working so late. He used to work late in the past, his company has peak periods I can understand, but lately, not only has he been working late much more often, when he's around, he also feels like he is not here. We don't talk, we don't communicate unless we need to, and the body language is like he is a stranger. So I want you to check on him, tell me whether he is really so busy that he has to leave the house so early, and come back so late, just because he says he has so much to do."

There was a pause, as if she was struggling with something. I couldn't be sure because the reflection from the window on her spectacles hid her eyes for an instant. "I want you to see if my husband is having something unusual on with one of his colleagues."

Ah, the pin drops. "What can you tell us about her, Mrs Tan?"

"Her name is Xiao Ping. My husband has felt distant for months, but I came across her name just last week when I got curious over some SMS messages that my husband had been receiving late into the night. We actually quarrelled about it and he blurted out a name. I don't know if he was careless or he just had nothing to hide. I checked his phone and the messages had been cleared, but I did find her name among his contacts. I can give you her number, in case you need it."

Is there something like "value add" when highly-educated women like this client give up climbing the corporate ladder to devote all their time to keeping the house clean and their kids out of trouble? Opportunity cost is much easier to tabulate: just bunch together former payslips and add the numbers, and there's your opportunity cost, money that one did not make as a result of doing time in the kitchen. But considering the number of children sexually abused, beaten or stuffed into ovens by domestic helpers – a small number admittedly, but no parent with a brain will derive any comfort from even that – having either husband or wife as full-time homemaker begins to make a lot of sense. And who knows, maybe a parent who actually had a career worth giving up in the first place would likewise have something worthwhile to pass down to the younger generation? Idle speculation, but not without grounds.

"Mrs Tan, we'll put a surveillance team on your husband for up to five days, or until we find something conclusive, whichever is earlier, and come back to you with our findings. Let me just say first, that we might not find anything at all. In that case, it's possible that your husband is not actually cheating on you, ok? And moreover, we will supply video and photos when it is possible to do so. We also do not do anything that compromises the safety of our investigators, and that of other road users during surveillance" I said.

I usually tell my clients that we might not get any results; it's not just to manage expectations. It also makes perfect sense because wanting to find something, and there being something to be found, are two separate things. It also helps to make this clear on the first meeting so clients are mentally more prepared and inclined to pay up come billing time. We should not confuse a negative result with not having a result in the first place.

Safety too, is also something we take very seriously. We may be mavericks for being in this trade in the first place; but we're not madmen.

"I understand. So five days will be good enough for you to ascertain if my husband is cheating."

Husbands running on auto-pilot. I suppose that's something that doesn't fall out of expectation if women continue to look for "career" in their prospective mates. No, it's not their fault that they prefer to date men who are more successful; these would after all, appear to be more secure choices in their ability to provide for the family. It's just that success has a tendency to spread in other areas too: a man who is successful in one aspect, likely has the qualities to succeed in others as well. Successful careers demand time from the family; that already is a primary source of distraction.

After we left the Tans, we decided that three from our agency would work on this assignment: Chandran, Alice and me. We've seen it too many times that a woman's world starts to unravel after they become full-time housewives. Their world becomes smaller as everything is built around the husband and the family, which can create paranoia and tension. But Mrs Tan did mention body language. That's subtle but at the same time, harder to hide. I had a hunch we'd be getting a positive result.

# CHAPTER 3

# FOLLOWING SOMEONE

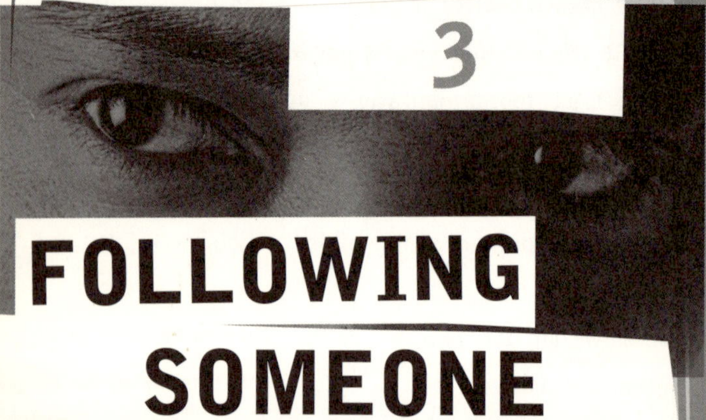

Have you ever been followed? It doesn't happen to me much, since I do most of the following.

Stalkers get some strange kick from following their intended, to satisfy an inexplicable obsession. They will go to extremes to do something that no one pays them to do – indeed they continue to shadow their obsession even under the threat of being sued, or hauled in by the police. One of these days, when I encounter a stalker case, I promise myself that I will thoroughly 'interrogate' these people when I get the chance. I might learn or thing or two, switching perspective between predator and prey. And perhaps if I get into their heads, I might also learn something about self and employee motivation: because for us investigators, tailing a subject, whether through a sea of humanity in a full-blown metropolis like Singapore, or in some remote place where we can scarcely take cover to conceal our presence, is a lot, a lot of hard work.

We have to keep the subject within sight as he changes buses or hops onto a train, as he amuses himself at a KTV, as he checks into a hotel room, and log everything he does, everyone he meets or talks to. Everything has to be recorded against a timescale, so our clients have as detailed as possible, an activity sheet of the person they have paid us to follow.

My colleague Chandran had done his stint the day before, following our subject Mr Tan to work. Now it was my turn to find out if it was going to be as gruelling as Chandran's full-page timesheet of just his morning commute alone, between 6:45 am and 9:30 am. Mr Tan is a migrating turtle.

In our archives, this particular case is labelled "Operation Bedok Reservoir" because that's where the subject stays and our trail starts there. However, it covers quite a few other areas. Just going to work from Bedok Reservoir to his office at Suntec City is tricky enough. But Mr Tan has connections, and detours.

He first takes a bus to Bedok MRT Station, takes a train to Paya Lebar MRT, gets on the Circle Line and takes a train to Serangoon MRT, gets on the North-East Line and alights at Punggol MRT; from here he rides an escalator up to the LRT station where he catches an LRT train to the Cove LRT Station. There he meets up with a female Chinese who appears to be in her 20s, slightly plump, with shoulder length hair. This presumably is Xiao Ping; thereafter our "co-subject".

From here, the two of them re-enact a virtual *Journey to the West* for sheer epic scope. They re-board the LRT and alight at the next stop; run – yes, run – across to take the LRT in the opposite direction to return to Punggol MRT, where they board a train for Dhoby Ghaut. They then change a train and terminate at Promenade MRT station, before riding an escalator up to Suntec City.

All this while, shadowing the subject and his companion, I am rushing in and out of trains, rushing between platforms, taking cover behind people, pillars, etc. At the same, I'm logging everything our subject does, by texting notes into my mobile phone. I'm a professional after all.

During this journey on public transport, there has been little public display of affection. Amidst the furious texting, I had taken a few snaps of them standing close together and talking, but rush hour commute in the morning is a battle, and no one's in the mood.

When they reach Suntec City, I can only read the subject and co-subject as best as I can. They split up for a short while: Mr Tan goes to buy canned drinks from the food court, while the co-subject gets buns from Crystal Jade Bakery. Then they walk together to the elevators, and board different lifts: Mr Tan to a lift serving the lower floors while the co-subject takes one for the upper floors. They don't even work in the same office?

Over the two mornings that we followed Mr Tan, he and the co-subject did the exact same thing: meeting at Cove LRT, coming to work at Suntec City together, buying bread and drinks, then heading to different lifts that will bring them to their respective offices on different floors. It was tedious beyond belief, and quite a feat for anyone to keep up, an effort of epic scale, just to get to work. I wonder how he even has any energy left to do his job, everyday. But I guess people just manage, somehow.

Over days three and four, we decided we'd tail the subject after work. On day three, one of my colleagues had stationed himself at Mr Tan's place of work at Suntec City at 5:30 pm. Nothing much happened; Mr Tan came out at 6:15 pm, followed by the co-subject and together they went to buy some pet food, before returning to their respective offices. Mr Tan did not have a pet at home.

My colleague waited further to possibly catch them when they knocked off but ten minutes later, only the co-subject came down, and she went home after ordering a takeaway at a fast-food restaurant. We don't normally follow a co-subject, as she is not our primary concern, but in this case, we wanted to ascertain if she was actually waiting for our subject to knock off together.

On day four, our patience paid off. At 5:30 pm, I planted myself outside Suntec Tower 1 where I would catch the subject coming out of his office. This time, Mr Tan came out at 6:23 pm, dressed in a white long-sleeved shirt, black pants and a grey necktie – so much for working late. He was looking at his watch and hung around the shops, and looked every bit like he was waiting for somebody. A minute later, co-subject Xiao Ping duly appeared, wearing a white dress and carrying a black handbag. I followed them as they walked slowly among the shops, entering some of them. They seemed like any other ordinary couple browsing the shops after work... which is to say, nothing too incriminating for me to photograph, since most couples are still quite reserved at a shopping centre.

I followed them to Esplanade MRT Station and into the train, alighting at Orchard MRT. And then it happened: on the escalator up Far East Plaza, Mr Tan and Xiao Ping were standing close together and talking. Then halfway through, he placed his hand casually around her waist. I was able to discreetly snap a picture on my phone.

They entered a Japanese restaurant to have dinner. I had no choice but to hang around the area, waiting for them to come out. Looking at the size and layout of the restaurant from the outside, I judged it'd be too difficult to observe the two of them in the restaurant itself; and when it was time to settle the bill and leave, it's hard to say if I would be able to settle the bill quickly and discreetly plant myself at an observation point as they leave. There were too many variables. They took an hour over dinner. I was starving.

After they left the restaurant, they took the overhead bridge and walked towards the hotel. Oh would there be action, I asked myself? But they made their way to the adjoining bar instead. Here, being a little darker than the restaurant, I was able to get myself a seat, order a beer that I paid for on the spot, and observe the two as they enjoyed their drinks.

It's true when they say that alcohol is a social lubricant. Soon subject and co-subject were comfortable enough, talking very closely and "intimacies were observed". That is all that goes into our files, there is no need to be more specific than that. But these words can mean quite a wide range of activities. As for our subject and co-subject, it was the touching of hands, light kisses and easy laughter. Nothing out of the ordinary if they were a married couple.

Their first attempt to catch the waiter's attention for the tab, as is usual in Singapore, went unnoticed. My personal theory is that local service staff are trained to avert eye contact so as not to render service as far as. But watching the couple very intently, I caught on straight away and left the bar to position myself properly to continue watching them as they come out.

They left for another pub, and continued with the easy familiarity that they had demonstrated in the first bar. This went on till just before 12 midnight, when they left the pub and hailed a cab. I followed them in another cab to the co-subject's house at Punggol. I thought Mr Tan would go up and stay a while but he didn't. The co-subject went up alone and Mr Tan continued home.

Basically we had enough information to ascertain that Mr Tan was indeed having more than friendly relations with the co-subject. But we would need more concrete information to make it more convincing. We had one more day to observe Mr Tan before we were due to give an account to our client Mrs Tan.

On day five, we were back to our stake out at Mr Tan's flat. It was a Friday, and we could see that his company also practised "Casual Friday": Mr Tan left his house at the usual time, but on this day was dressed in a T-shirt and jeans and carried a sling bag. Instead of his usual route, he walked to a bus stop and took a bus to Tampines. I wonder if he suspected his wife was having him followed, because he kept turning his head to look around. Well, even if sees us, we look different from the day before.

From Tampines, he crossed a few streets to another bus stop, where he boarded a second bus and ended up at Punggol. He was not making this easy, with all this walking and boarding. We knew that Punggol was where the co-subject stayed, from following her home on two nights. Indeed Mr Tan went to the block where the co-subject stayed and sat at the void deck for a while, seemingly waiting for someone.

It's not a good idea to observe someone from too close, especially the void deck, which has nothing. Residents walking by will get suspicious, so we were actually observing Mr Tan from the adjacent block's void deck. Here, some youngsters were hanging around at the marble table and chairs that we wanted as a suitable observation point. When it comes to this, intimidation is often better than courtesy.

I put on my meanest face and approached the group: "Oi! What are you kids hanging around here? Don't you have school?" The brats scrammed, not before assuring my team that they were not up to any mischief. It doesn't always work as we intend, but intimidation is also one of the tools we use as we respond to situations. Works on all kinds of people, from kids to adults. It just takes experience to guess who it'll work on, and how to wring it. Otherwise it backfires.

We actually expected that Mr Tan was waiting for the co-subject to come down from her flat, but instead, he got up and entered the lift. We had already ascertained the unit number of Xiao Ping's flat when one of us followed her back the other night. One of my colleagues rushed to the block while I took the lift up to observe the unit on the adjacent block. From the adjacent block, I could see that the front grill gate was locked but that the main door was open, and no one was in the living room. I instructed my colleague to approach the unit. He confirmed that he could not see anyone in the living room, but that there was a dog inside the unit. So that was what the pet food from the other day was for.

I put my colleague on standby, and when he returned to the unit more than an hour and a half later, at 11:40 am, nothing had changed, the door was still open and no one was in the living room. They could only be in the bedroom, then; the unit wasn't large enough to have much else.

So, he didn't go to work on Friday. This was news to his wife too, when we spoke to her the following Monday while he was at work. "You followed them up to the apartment?" Mrs Tan didn't say much as we gave her a report of our findings, nodding on occasion and generally looking thoughtful.

"I'm afraid so. We have a video of the both of them entering her flat, and they were in the flat for more than an hour, no one was in the living room," I said, as I concluded our briefing.

She would have much to face up to, and her kids too. If I bothered too much with the kind of ripples our work has on the personal lives of our clients, it would become impossible to do it. And we do have a job to do, one that people pay us to do well, because they have a desire, and in some cases a right, to know. The information we uncover can wreck homes; but we're not the wreckers.

# CHAPTER 4

# PROJECT BIG SWEEP

Catching cheating spouses is something but we also do corporate work for businesses. There are also a great number of cheaters here, be they business partners, potential tie-ups or even trusted employees. Can people trust people? Well at some level, things grind to a halt if there is no trust. Yet, to deceive the other party for some benefit is primal human nature, something which we need to guard against.

When you have a hunch that something is wrong, yet no crime seems to have been committed – metaphorically or literally, there is no smoking gun and no body – who can you call? The police have better things to do. They cannot dispatch a team every time someone has a hunch that trouble is around the corner. But you can call us. For a fee, private investigators will find out what you need to know, beyond what you are able to suss out by searching through your web browser.

Not that I'm belittling the usefulness of the Internet. On the contrary, we use it prettty much as any business or individual; we just have lots of legwork to go with it.

One stressed-out business owner approached us when she could no longer ignore the warning signs to her business. Yet there just wasn't any firm grounds she could get hold of to approach the police for help. It's like an internal haemorrhage. You are bleeding and losing vitality from within, yet there's no bruise on the surface to tell you something is wrong.

"I suspect my senior sales manager is doing something behind my back. I've been getting calls from some of my old clients that they are being approached by some company that I previously never heard of, which is quoting some prices and products quite close to our own. Yet when

I ask around our clients and even some of our competitors that we are on good terms with, no one knows anything. I have a feeling it's an inside job, but I have no concrete information and don't know where to start," said Amy.

Amy runs a small business selling and installing clothes drying racks for apartments and houses of all sizes.

On paper it looks like a small-scale business, but volumes can be very substantial when a client – say, a developer – orders in bulk for its residential project. And the company offered something for every budget, from simple portable racks that could be brought in and out of the house depending on the weather, to pretty complex built-in systems that were fully automated. The top-of-the line racks could be lowered and raised out of the way at the touch of a button, and came with their own spotlight and fan units to facilitate indoor drying. There must be hundreds of small and medium sized enterprises (SME) like hers offering all kinds of innovative goods and services which do not have the resources and systems in place to protect their businesses from unscrupulous activities and persons.

"Why do you suspect your sales manager?" I asked. It never hurts to find out as much as you can, then do the filtering later.

"Whoever is hijacking our business seems to be targeting only us. From what some of my clients who were approached tell me, they have good knowledge about our prices and products. My sales manager Sundram would have this kind of knowledge, and he also seems busier than I expect, from the amount of business he is bringing in," said Amy.

This wasn't much to go on, but actually having an individual identified is a start. A start could always lead somewhere, to a trail we can follow to the end. I told Amy what we proposed to do: "We will set up a trap purchase on Sundram. I will pose as a potential client for your company, and we'll see if he tries to steal my business for another company. If a purchase is made, we will have a paper trial, and the proof that you need to take any action that you may require." You cannot prove a weasel without bait.

We managed to convince Amy that in the absence of anything concrete beyond a hunch, a trap purchase was the logical way forward. A trap purchase is something I had done on occasion while I was in the police force; it's a most aggressive, get-your-hands-dirty tactic to have direct interaction with your subjects. Much can be read from this interaction, and it's in principle similar but a little simpler than following an ant trail to its nest. On her part, Amy would lend us a mobile phone from which to initiate the transaction, as well as an empty apartment in Hougang for us to use.

The next day, I gave Sundram a call. I told him I wished to install a particular model of drying rack in a flat. He sounded friendly on the phone, and quoted me $750 with installation. We made an appointment to meet at the Hougang flat later in the same evening. We had to make this deal work. If he didn't bite, we could always set up another fake buy with another apartment, led by another colleague. But that would be troublesome. Much would depend on the meeting later on. I would have to make it clear to Sundram somehow, that I was "flexible", just like him – assuming his boss Amy was right in suspecting he had been less than honest with the company.

Of course I didn't just go meet Sundram at the Hougang flat. There were already so many variables which could happen during the deal. It is always our job to be as prepared as possible, to iron out the uncertainties as far as we can beforehand. This could be as mundane as finding the flat that Amy had arranged for our use, and making sure the keys that she gave us, worked. The whole thing could fall apart if later on during the meeting, I had any problem locating the unit that I was supposed to buy something for, and if the keys to my own apartment didn't work.

Having satisfied myself that everything was in order, I called Sundram again, and we met at the void deck. I disliked him right away. Which meant this fake trap purchase had a very high chance of success. Sundram carried himself with a touch of self-importance, was over-friendly and greasy; in other words, Sundram appeared a salesman's salesman. I must say that did not sound flattering, and is indeed somewhat prejudiced against sales as a profession.

Let me clarify that I have every respect for sales and marketing folk, and for good reason. Without salesmanship and salespersons, goods, ideas, services, just could not pass as smoothly as they must in a proper functioning society and economy. What I meant was that from the looks of things, Sundram fit right up there with the stereotype of the extra savvy, smooth talker (who imagined himself to be a smooth talker, anyway) who was ever ready to cut deals. Employers hire these people looking for deal-making supremos, but they also have to face up to the prospect that unless these dealmakers also had a deeply seated work ethic, they could be just as ready to cut deals at the expense of the company, since all that mattered to them was not the company that employed them per se, but their own selves.

"Sundram, I'm Robert, we spoke on the phone. Nice to

meet you, shall we proceed to the flat?" We shook hands, and exchanged pleasantries. I learned from Sundram that he had been doing sales for more than 15 years, and spent the last four years at the present company selling clothes drying rack systems to individuals and businesses, that he was the go-to guy for everything, from sales to even installation, since it was a small company and he was one of the more senior, if not the most senior person in the company.

"So Robert, how did you find us?" We were making our way to the unoccupied unit on the 11th floor, supplied by Amy for this sting operation, and making small talk to feel each other out.

"From the Internet!" I said with a laugh. It was important to keep things a little chummy. "I was very impressed by the looks of your product range, and the video demonstrations on the webpage were very well done and convincing."

"You know we did the video ourselves? You see my boss doing the presentation but I was the one holding the camera. Are you buying our clothesline for your own flat?"

Sundram was quite a large man. Our work doesn't "get physical" if you know what I mean, but I always size up people and situations by instinct, just in case things go horribly wrong. After all, I'm entering into a non-public space with a large-built man I am trying to entrap. Oh, the irony, if things turn sour. But I've done this countless times. Confidence is key.

"No, this is for my boss. It's his flat. He bought it recently and asked me to get it furnished." It's important to supply just enough information to keep things afloat, but never more than that.

Instead of giving the other party information to analyse and piece together, I always try to distract them with the most distracting thing: themselves! I make them talk about themselves, their hobbies, likes, ambitions; how they feel the world can be a better place, if it comes to that. It's true what some people say about opinions, likening them to a rude but necessary body-part: everyone's got one. And some types love to share. Sundram included. By the time we reached the apartment, we were getting along pretty well.

Imagine how clumsy things would have been if the key didn't work, or if I had trouble finding the unit, walking up and down wrong corridors. None of that happened because I had prepared early. "This is where I want you to install the Model A clothesline that you quoted me for," I told Sundram, pointing to the kitchen window.

Sundram was quiet for longer than an instant as he looked at the window. I could almost see the wheels turning in his head, making phantom calculations that he thought was only visible to him. "I have to remove the central metal piece of the window frame to install the Model A," Sundram said after making a fine show of inspecting the window frame.

"Cannot, lah. You know this is not my flat but it belongs to my boss. He doesn't allow me to do this kind of major thing." I was myself making a fine show of seeming troubled. Good planning, and so far so good...

"But I cannot install the Model A if you don't let me remove the central piece on the window frame," Sundram said. After a pregnant pause, and seeing that I was looking a little troubled, Sundram spoke again. "Tell you what. How about I install a custom-made model for you? I won't have to remove the centre piece on your window frame, and instead of the $750 that I quoted you, this custom-made model only costs $520. But it's from another company."

"With installation?" I looked my most incredulous self. This is the beauty of information and planning, if I say so myself. There are beautiful accidents, but no one needs the heart attack when it comes to my line of work. Everything proceeding according to plan was the best, and if anything outside of expectation came up, it was only welcome if it served the unanticipated hand to move the plan along, like a train on rails. Diversions can be frightfully costly, in more ways than one.

"Yes with installation and everything. But this model is from another company." Sundram was rising to the occasion beautifully. He was taking the bait, and a little smug at it, too.

"A discount even, that's great! But can you do me a favour? It's no difference to you, can you still invoice me as $750, but I pay you $520? I can claim the difference. You know how little we guys make running around all over the place doing rubbish?" I was suggesting something that was of course, under normal circumstances, utterly dishonest. Criminal even, though the 'c' word is something quite sensitive in my profession where we sometimes have to skirt rather close around the rules without breaking them. But showing my willingness to do a shady deal brought me down to Sundram's level, in his eyes. It put us on the same page, and gave him assurance to believe that I had the self-interest to be discreet.

"No problem, I can do it for you. I get business, and you get something for your effort also: it's a win-win situation!" Sundram declared with no small measure of triumph.

This was all going according to well-laid plans, which also underlines the importance of working with our clients. It was our client Amy who told us that their systems could not be installed to the particular type of window frame in the flat she supplied without first removing the centre piece of the window frame. And we designed this trap purchase based on information that Amy's own clients gave her, that someone was offering customised models that did not require modifications for installation around this type of window frame.

"Okay, thanks a lot. No need to say, we keep this between ourselves. Got more business, I definitely look for you!" I assured Sundram. Chummy. I waited for Sundram to take some measurements, and after locking up we proceeded to the void deck; I had to set some ink to the deal.

"Sundram, thanks I think we will be happy working together. When can you come to install the clothesline?"

"Today is Thursday; I need to get the stock, and also to go back and custom make a frame to make it fit. I'll come down this Sunday to install the thing? Can you also give me a deposit first?"

"I don't have enough cash on hand to give you a deposit. Tell you what, I will transfer the full amount to you tomorrow. Give me your particulars. I'm doing this over the Internet, so I'll need the account number, as well as the account name." Didn't I say we love the Internet?

Sundram wrote his wife's bank account details on a piece of paper and handed it to me. Evidence, in his own handwriting. I pocketed it carefully.

The following day, I went to the bank and transferred the money to the account Sundram gave me, over the counter. I wasn't really going to use the Internet. And I wanted the transcript.

On Sunday, I met with Sundram at the Hougang flat. He had traded the long-sleeve shirt and slacks for a pair of rather worn coveralls. I was jovial: "Eh, you're a senior manager and you're really doing the installation yourself? And wearing coveralls – very professional! Where are your people?"

"We do everything la. I sell, and I also measure, and install.

And Sunday some more." We chatted as Sundram got on with the installation, during which time he had to make a few trips to the van that he came in, getting supplies and all. Throughout, he kept emphasizing that his product – "his" was let slip – was very high quality and safe, from the UK.

"You don't worry about this product. Though it's cheaper, my product is very safe. It meets all the regulations, and it's made in England."

"Sundram, you're a very capable guy. You want more business? My boss has some projects coming up and we will need more installations. You interested?"

"Sure, of course. Let me know when you have other opportunities."

The installation took about an hour to complete. I wanted more. "Sundram, can you do a video demo that I can show my boss? Show him that we did a good job la. I brought the camera already."

Sundram readily agreed and I recorded the demo in HD living colour. Now we've got a payment record for $520, a handwritten note to connect this payment to the person we were investigating, the product installed in our scam flat, and a video of the subject himself on a song and dance. As we parted after installation, Sundram also handed me a receipt, from ABC Company, complete with company registration number, for $750.

But I wanted more. Or more precisely, to make sure there wasn't more. I pressed him for a further quote. "Remember to send me a quotation. We have some new projects coming up, and the volume will be more, so give me a good price." We shook hands and parted.

The following Tuesday, when I had still not received a quotation from Sundram after a reminder the previous day, I called him again.

"What happened, Sundram, how come still no quotation from you?"

"Sorry ah, I've been busy."

Had he caught on to something? It didn't matter at this point, he had not only bitten off the bait, he had already swallowed. But I turned it up a notch anyway, just to be sure.

"Sundram, this is big ah. I didn't tell you the other day because the details still not firm. Now I can tell you, we need a quote for 46 more installations!"

"Whoa that's a lot!" Sundram was getting interested.

Just to thicken it a bit: "And I want a referral fee for $150 for each unit. Can be done?" This was the essential handshake I think. Honour among thieves is not honour per se, but a common interest in all that dishonesty!

"Okay brother, no problem. Thanks for the business, we're happy working together," said Sundram.

"Okay thanks, that's good. But this is a big project, so for the records, it looks better if I get a quote from a private limited company with a paid-up capital. How?"

"No problem. I actually just started my own company recently. I can use that to issue you a formal quotation."

"Excellent! Look forward to it. Send it to me by 3 pm!" I hung up, mighty pleased. So there was a deeper bottom after all.

At 2:40 pm, I received a quotation from Master Company Private Limited. It was all legitimate on the surface. That meant names could be traced, all available in the public domain. My client's hunch had been right. Now she had the paper trail to hit back. Her senior sales manager, in collusion with others, had been stealing business from her through selling compatible and competing products through not one but two distinct companies. Through us, our client Amy had just bought herself a lot of rope.

# CHAPTER 5

# PROJECT BIG SWEEP: FALLOUT

A fallout of some kind was almost a certainty, given the way we had so utterly wrapped up Project Big Sweep. The previous case of the senior sales manager at a clothes drying systems company stealing business from his own employer, had been a very good success, and the haul of evidence was, by any standard, very complete. We had all the paper and rubber stamping we needed, and even a video of the subject himself, unrehearsed, uncoerced!

Moonlighting has its proper limits – as does liberty, money and pretty much all else. But our client Amy also found herself with another problem. Our cunning trap purchase had indeed dug up such a lot of rot that she had to re-think a lot of things, and make decisions about what to do with all that unpleasant information. How much has this parasitic betrayal – breach of trust, if you prefer – cost her business, and for how long?

The subject didn't just sell cheaper products at a slightly lower price and skimmed off the difference, he didn't even ask to share the price difference I pocketed because he had already made enough profit from selling the product to me. And not only that, he had even set up a private limited company, with all the regulatory requirements that entailed, with a substantial paid-up capital. We knew this from the second quote he gave me for the mass order. This was no small-change palm greasing but a pretty well-oiled operation that had been doing a pretty brisk trade, right under my client's nose!

The loss in dollar terms will take some effort to trace and tabulate, but what about the cost to the reputation of her company within the related sectors, and her own personal standing as a businesswoman among her fellow entrepreneurs? We had given her a lot of rope as I have said. But perhaps she had also been presented with a dilemma as to who to hang with it.

I do not mean to advertise the necessity of my chosen profession, but to know is better than not to know. It's like medication delivering the cure with side effects, but we'd be fools not to take the medication anyway. And in this case, it's better to get over the pain of being made the fool and get the professionals to uncover the people who have been doing the fooling, thinking they can get away with it.

I wasn't very surprised when Amy called me again a few days after we had handed her all the information pertaining to her (soon to be former) senior sales manager.

"Your agency did a very good job on the assignment I gave you."

That sounded like a compliment. I couldn't resist: "It was our duty; you pay for quality."

"I want to appoint your agency to continue the work. You will be the right people to do it."

"There's more?" We weren't paid to dig all the way the previous time, just to find enough dirt on her employee

Sundram. But setting up a private limited company to do the siphoning led me to expect that he wasn't alone. This call must be about rounding up the rest of the gang.

"Yes. I looked up the private listed company that issued you the second invoice. I got a shock when I went to check up who are directors behind the company. It's not just Sundram, but also my accounts clerk! She does the accounting, the figures... and all this while she has been stealing from my company together with my sales manager! What can you guys do?"

"We expected there to be more people colluding with Sundram, but your accounts clerk as the other person involved in the scheme is striking pretty close to home. We can question her and see where the trail leads." It's "her" because there are no male accounts clerks. I tend to believe that.

The next afternoon, I went down to my client's place of business, dressed in rolled up white long-sleeve shirt and black pants; a lanyard with card holder stuffed into my front breast pocket. The idea was to give the impression that I work in an office of some importance: a government office. And coupled with my short-cropped hair and very rough-looking face, I could only be a cop! Well, I was a police investigator before, so looking like one is never a problem. It's the way you look at people and the way you carry yourself. Walk around like you have a badge that holds some real power, and you will have a subtle swagger that people can find intimidating when you choose to project it. And for this afternoon, I had every intention to project every ounce of intimidation I could muster.

I was also armed with files and papers: everything serious is always contained in files and papers. Especially cardboard files often associated with old-fashioned government ministries, not the brightly covered plastic folders that so-called modern offices in hip industry sectors like to use. Every little detail is important, and carrying dull old cardboard file folders help to project the image that the person you're trying to intimidate is in deep, deep trouble. I know, we're wicked.

Amy my client had also given me information about her accounts clerk. Maria was a Philippine national and Singapore Permanent Resident. She had been working in Singapore for five years, and must have found the standard – or rather the cost – of living quite high. So high as to resort to robbing her own employer blind.

I practically stormed into the office – at least for show

– with my colleague Alice. A female colleague is needful when dealing with a female subject. It's a precaution one should never neglect, as you never know what can happen. This is real life, not a simulated scenario at some police academy. And we approached the subject at her cubicle.

In my most officious voice: "Mary Jane Jamoyot?"

"Yes? What is this about?"

"My name is Heng Ping Kai, I am an investigator and this is my colleague. A complaint has been filed against you. Can you please come into the conference room with us." I had flashed my card, and put it back into my breast pocket, but not too quickly, just smoothly.

Interesting thing about reading faces is how messages like fear, panic, anger or joy can flit across in an instant. It's not static like letters on a page. What I just saw was a trace of panic. A person with nothing to hide is near impossible to squeeze. There just isn't any leverage, unless he or she is just born extra timid. But a guilty conscience is a different thing altogether: guilt is a lever of unease.

Mary Jane must have been waiting for a day like this, when the scheme hatched with her colleague Sundram the sales manager would eventually be found out. There was panic, and a moment's debate on how to handle our request. One tactic was to go on the defensive, and try to bluff one's way through with a blusterous "Who the hell are you?" The other was to come quietly with us and perhaps stall for time and hope for the best. As some of her other colleagues were already starting to peep over their cubicle partitions, and the boss Amy was also looking at this whole scene in full view of her employees through her office window, Mary Jane decided it was wiser not to create a bigger scene and come quietly with us.

Also, when I introduced myself, I left out "private". I was just "investigator", which is what I am, I'm not lying. But it doesn't hurt if the subject thought Alice and I were cops, with handcuffs ready. We didn't have handcuffs, just a videocam.

As soon as the door was closed behind us, the interrogation began. "We know about what you did with Sundram. We have all the evidence we need, to establish the fact that the both of you started Master Company Private Limited, while you were still working here, selling compatible and competitive products against the interest of your present employer. What do you have to say for yourself?"

She was turning a little pale. Because our client had not yet called the police, Sundram still did not have a clue that he had starred in video that was going to be used against him in court. Mary Jane also had not expected trouble until Alice and I showed up at the office with that imperious, serious-business look about us. She was like the proverbial doe, suddenly caught in the headlights of a rampaging Mercedes Benz, three-pointed star bonnet sight aimed dead centre. Panic was good, I could use it. I am sure if I had dug further, we would probably find some kind of special relationship between Mary Jane and Sundram as well, beyond partners of a scam. But this private aspect of their relationship was not directly relevant to case, but still useful in the background because it made Mary Jane all the more panicky and jumpy, giving her much more to hide. Good leverage.

"You have the right not to say anything. You can even leave this office right now. But I advise you, we have all the evidence we need, we are just giving you a chance to save yourself more trouble than is necessary," I prodded her a bit, cause she was visibly upset but still hadn't said a word. And it was also important that we had advised her of her right to choose not to cooperate with us. An important point of procedure. Just in case we are accused of unjust intimidation. You can intimidate all you want, just don't get caught doing it unjustly. You can say "You have the right to..." with as much malice and threat as you can project to scare the subject silly, but you just got to remember to follow proper procedure. I let the tension build a little more.

Then judging the right moment, I raised my voice, "Are you sure you have nothing to say!" And with well-calibrated violence, I accidentally dropped the file I was carrying (quite a thick one for effect) on the table, and I made sure she could see the Xeroxed copies of receipts, invoices, and most importantly, the several pages of video screen captures of good ol' Sundram demonstrating the use of the very product they were selling. I watched as her eyes widened and teared.

"I am so sorry! I am so sorry we sold the products and it harmed this company. I am so sorry!" The tears came thick and fast, and between sobs, more of the scheme and details came out. They had been running the scheme for a year, and working from the knowledge and contacts gained from working for my client, they had been able to run a profitable business. That goes without saying. An illegal business has to be profitable otherwise it cannot justify the unfair advantages gained illegally, and it also has to be lucrative enough to be worth the risk of getting found out and punished.

Mary Jane was in full cooperation mode. She probably felt better now anyway. She didn't seem utterly greedy, I had a hunch she went along with the scam under strong persuasion. As the accounts person in the company, she was certainly very important for the scheme to work so well: a lot of financial and client data passed through her hands.

"Do you have additional documents about your setup that you can show me here?" I dialled down the menace in my voice a few notches. Capturing and responding to the dynamics of the circumstances is the key in any situation. Now was the time for a little empathy.

"Yes, they are on my computer." She led me to her computer and showed me her files, even her personal emails. I could not help but notice, some email exchanges with Sundram were way friendly. That was probably the key reason behind her involvement in all this, before the profits provided additional momentum.

This probable relationship was not our direct concern, but the fact that the company had been set up by Sundram, her and another party. Mary Jane also revealed that she had set up a warehouse cum office in Sin Ming Industrial Estate, just 10 minutes away, which she volunteered to take us to.

It was after 7 pm by the time we set off. It was not a standalone warehouse but a good-sized business unit, probably around two thousand square feet. I stationed Alice to be on watch outside while I followed Mary Jane into the unit. This is not unlike entering a cave, because we never know what's in there, so always best to have someone on lookout, to dial 999 if necessary!

True enough, when we entered, there was a Filipino at a desk using the computer. Mary Jane explained that he was a friend of hers, then they conversed a little in machine gun Tagalog. I didn't understand a word.

Mary Jane proceeded to show me around the unit, and like a tourist, I took it all down on video – very handy things – all the while being very conscious of the guy at the computer.

As we were about to leave, the guy actually approached us and confronted me in an aggressive manner, asking me what I was doing taking videos of the premises, and in a raised voice. I didn't want trouble, and escalation is not always wise since this is not a public place. Still, two could play at this.

"What is your business here?" I demanded.

"I work here. Why shouldn't I be here? Who are you to ask? Who do you think you are?"

"This warehouse is under OUR investigation. I ask you again, what exactly do you do here? Why were you using the computer?" My voice was getting louder than his. "Investigation" is always a big word for those who know in themselves that they have something to be investigated about.

I got on the offensive when he quietened down.

"Show me your ID!" To which the man duly complied. Other private investigators might rely a lot on electronic gadgets, but nothing battery operated can help in situations like this. Battling wits and will is a skill.

I took down his particulars, then verified with Mary Jane that he wasn't actually an employee at the company she had set up.

"Mister, you are not an employee here. Are you an over-stayer in this country? It's a very serious offense."

What a change in attitude that caused. As if a physical switch had been flipped somewhere, the man's demeanour and posture did a dramatic 180-degree turn. He got all humble and meek and apologetic. He actually started to plead with me not to turn him in. We had got what we came for, mission accomplished, and I didn't want him to turn desperate and do something violent so I just left it at that.

When we returned to my client's office, yet more video footage was added to the cache of evidence for the police and courts to recover as much as was possible for my client. At least when it came time to seizing the assets, they would have a video record of what the conspirators had amassed. My client would still have lost something from this whole affair. The work of our agency was to help our client salvage as much of the stolen property as possible, including her dignity. And perhaps also equip her with better procedures, management skills and intuition to prevent similar things from happening in the future. Another happy – and wiser – client served.

# CHAPTER 6

# PROJECT YACHT CLUB "CHEATERS ALL"

Do women cheat? This question can only ever be asked rhetorically. No one asking this should be dumb enough to really expect an answer. Of course women cheat. They are no less human than men; and if we are often enough labelled the lying cheating bastards that we sometimes are, we cannot in good conscience suppose women to be any less. If there is a lying bone or organ in our body that makes liars of men, women would have it, too.

Not all the cases we take on concern adultery of some sort, but usually, these cases are quite thick on human drama, because the currency in the relationships here is not economic as in the corporate cases, but affection. The loss of it. The results of our investigations in these cases can change lives. The truth can be especially disruptive as whole families are violently torn apart. I do not exaggerate. We are talking about investigating the most intimate of relationships, the ones around which lives are defined, and planned. In fact, I would venture to say that in most cases, even before the first report is filed, the nature of the relationship had already undergone an irreversible change by the very act of picking up the phone and calling our office to tail a spouse.

From that moment of resolve, trust had been shattered and the relationship had crossed a milestone, a mile marker towards terminal point.

I remember the case of this husband who suspected his wife of having an affair with her boss. An ordinary-looking couple living in a HDB flat, with a kid, and sharing a modest little car between them which they drive on certain days – it cuts fuel and mileage if you don't drive everyday.

They don't do too badly. He's an engineer in middle

management; she takes care of the kid and the household while working part-time on certain days as a clerk at a neighbourhood clinic.

What could be more mundane than that. But marital problems – while potentially life-changing – are at the same time the most mundane things in the world! Through the work I do, I have come to view any marriage as a marriage under threat. Like a piano suspended in the air, just biding its time for the spectacular drop. That's what marriage is, and that's why I don't understand the fanfare that comes with it. Perhaps to remind the couple that it's going to be quite a challenge keeping the marriage afloat against its natural tendency to sink? Well, in that case, the joy of the proceedings is the mystery, then.

"Mr Heng, I think my wife is having an affair." No time to mince words, eh? Consultation is not really charged by the hour, so my clients don't really need to rush into their stories. But some of them are in a hurry, sometimes.

"We can look into it. We can have a team to monitor her. What makes you think she's having an affair?" The thing about not rushing into their stories: a good investigator always listens. If the PI you're thinking of hiring looks so seasoned that he or she looks on the brink of dozing off from having heard the story too many times, change your service provider. Stories may seem alike, but the individuals involved are different and how can you put your trust in someone who has no empathy for your cause? You're paying good money, and beyond experience and skill, empathy is also something that should be included in the price. That's my opinion, anyway.

"My wife seems very distant these days. I don't have any concrete sign on hand, and I am not looking for anything very solid. I ask her about it and she just denies. It's very hard to talk to her that way, and yet I cannot deny to myself that there is something wrong. I believe her phone is private so I cannot bring myself to check it, but I think it's okay to follow her around a bit. I want to know what she gets up to these days, and would like to follow her around a bit; but I've got a job to do." An engineer, everything is a problem waiting for the right solution. Well, he could do much worse than calling us, you know. Like listening to his friends. Friends are invaluable as listening ears, till they venture well-intentioned advice. There are exceptions, but not many that I have personally encountered.

"Of course, we'd be happy to help. We will follow her, and report back to you with our findings. Then you can decide what you want to do from there."

Mr Tan was methodical through and through. Before we concluded our discussion about fees, and the usual conditions about non-guarantee of results, and putting the safety of our staff and the general public first above all else, he had given us quite a lot of information to work from: a photo of his wife, her workplace address, as well as a pretty good general description of Dr Chew (her boss, with whom he suspects the wife of having an affair) and the make, model, colour and licence plate of the car Dr Chew drove. He could work for us!

A large part of a private investigator's work is waiting, waiting, waiting. Waiting for the subject to come off work, waiting while they do their shopping, waiting while they watch a movie, hang out or eat a meal. This list is as endless as the sum of one's daily activities. And then, these long periods of tedium are punctuated by very quick, unexpected transitions where we really have to use our wits to keep on the trail, or to respond to new situations that arise with no warning.

Though we had good leads from Mr Tan, tailing his wife was unexpectedly difficult. She and her husband might be distant, but she sure seemed to have gleaned a clue that she was being watched. Every so often, she would turn around and look around, to see if she was being followed.

We had to post different staff to tail her at different points. Once she drove around the whole estate before going back to the house. Another time, walking between housing block flats, she suddenly ran up the stairs and actually managed to shake off one of my colleagues by hiding and descending via another stairwell. What is this woman thinking? I had to call her husband to ascertain matters!

"Does your wife know she is being followed? Do you know that she has been actively evading us?" I felt I had to understand the situation a little better by speaking to my client directly. It helps me work more effectively.

"Not really. I didn't tell her. Actually we don't talk much these days." Mr Tan was a little surprised that his wife had been pulling the ninja on us. It does suggest she has much to hide, but it could also be just a person being plain finicky.

But what would that make us if we couldn't even tail a housewife? In any case, we managed to tail her to the office on a few occasions and studied her movements from there. Very queer. On certain workdays, she would drive to the yacht club after work, and have dinner with her boss. The restaurant is open to the public so getting in for us is no problem – we just can't park where the members do. But neither can our subject. So every time they eat at the yacht club when they are ready to leave, the boss always walks to the subject's car first and drives it over to where she is waiting outside the restaurant lobby. Peculiar but gentlemanly, no?

During the meal itself, though their conduct never boils over into something inappropriate – they are at a restaurant, after all – it is not difficult for my colleagues and I to see that there is some chemistry between them. Fortunately, we managed to capture this on video and photographs, while watching and waiting from a table a discreet distance away. This takes practice, of course. And a nice camera hidden within a case disguised as a clutch bag – the type uncles love to carry, which always seems to be full of money, that don't look out of place when left on the table. In any case, you cannot be so intent on photographing the subject that you take your eyes off the service staff.

And then one day, it does boil over. As usual, they had eaten a very late dinner at the yacht club. What is usual here is of course unusual. There is little usual about two adults routinely having dinner past nine, who are each married to other people who are not on the invite list.

My colleague hurries off to the main gate to wait just as we see the motions of getting the bill. If they go off together or both drive off in their respective cars to a common destination, my colleague would be on hand to tail them, from his bike parked at the main gate. I chose to follow the couple since this time, they both walked to the car park together instead of him getting her car for her.

And there indeed, in the car, there was the odd fumbling. I caught the couple continuing the "conversation" they couldn't have under the bright lights in the restaurant. Well, a snap. And then I was off.

Yes, it was messy. But it's my client's mess. He paid to know, and now he knows.

# CHAPTER 7

# PROJECT PJ

"PJ" doesn't stand for pyjamas though it very well could. It stands for Petaling Jaya, a township just a little outside of Kuala Lumpur. It irks me a little when I read of people saying such nasty things about Malaysia and even when they are in a good mood, the nastiness gives way to an even more annoying attitude of being downright patronising. No, I am not a Malaysian, but what does it matter if we are or are not? This is but a piece of paper? The distinction becomes all the more arbitrary when we consider that we used to be one country; and even today, we still maintain so many links with Malaysia, be they familial, business or even amorous.

I am sure it is no leap of imagination that a fair number (unreported, obviously; this is not something that our mighty national statistics department has any interest nor ability to assess) of Singapore men have mistresses in Malaysia. You can even say it's a little like Shenzhen for the Hong Kongers. But perhaps not so blatant, because Malaysia has much more besides to offer than Shenzhen beyond being a safe harbour for fantasy adventures.

But speaking of safe harbour, it isn't very safe anyway. The cost is higher – because we need to travel, and also liaise with local resources – but we also handle cases where a spouse is suspected of fun and games when he (or she, as the case may be) is supposed to be on business across the causeway. This is where PJ comes in. Enter Mr Hock, aged 38. Reasonably successful, not too bad looking; works in sales so he meets a lot of people, very sociable, and also makes many trips to Malaysia where many of his clients are. All five Cs accounted for, but women who go for these charismatic, and ambitious fellows also tend to suffer the sixth C as well: concubines. But not in every case.

From information supplied by the wife, my Malaysian counterpart Alvin and I arrived at ABC Coatings Sdn Bhd in Petaling Jaya, Malaysia.

We were looking for Mr Hock's (our subject) car in the parking lot. There was security but a little pocket money is usually enough to keep the guy at the guard post quiet. This happens not just in Malaysia. We are in the information business and in these civilised times, information, in Singapore and Malaysia, at the hotel, KTV, restaurant, etc. is bought if not bullied off people who have it. If you're a cop in certain countries, you might try beating it out of someone, too. But Singapore and Malaysia are mighty civilised, relatively speaking.

We made two runs round the company parking lot without sighting the subject's car, so we drove to the Petaling Jaya Hilton where we knew our subject was staying. Alvin drove, of course. His little Myvi, originally a harmless 1.2 litre hatchback, had been spiced with a turbo, and went very well. If we had to tail any car, this would be up to it in most cases. Though there's a little monster of an engine in the hood, there are no more body kits than usual to draw unnecessary attention to it as it's a work vehicle. I noted with approval that Alvin had even been very restrained when it came to stickers. Just something about being kind to animals, nothing more.

We found the subject's car at the hotel parking lot. We just couldn't find the subject. "I'll go make some enquiries,"

Alvin said and approached the concierge. If this were Singapore, I would be the one talking to the concierge but here in Malaysia, we got Alvin because he knows people here. This is the home turf advantage. That way, you know who to pay to get what.

Alvin came to me as I was having lunch at the hotel restaurant. "I've confirmed that our subject is staying here, at Room 1061. He's not in at the moment, so we wait?"

"Yeah. You wait for him and let me know when he comes back. I'll go get us a room." Paid for by my client, of course. Sharing the same hotel has many advantages. At least it doesn't look so suspicious for us to lurk about, since we are also guests. We would have more reason to tip the bell hops and other staff to get our way.

That day was quite uneventful, though not without incident. With Alvin staked out at the lobby, I did not get a report from him till almost 10 pm. Mr Hock returned to the hotel in a cream-coloured SUV driven by a female Chinese. Alvin managed to take a picture, and followed our subject up to his room and was on standby where he could observe the door. When our subject still didn't come out till 4 am, I asked Alvin to halt the surveillance and come back to our room a floor below. That's how hard we work.

The next morning, our subject was in a jolly mood. We were staked out at the lobby at 7 am, and our subject was out of his room at 8 am, chatting happily on the phone. Next he had a chummy conversation with an Indian driver – whom we couldn't identify – at the driveway, before heading to the hotel restaurant for breakfast. There, he met with a Chinese man and they had a discussion. Probably work-related. We took photos anyway, just to be sure. But with work out of the way, our subject went up to his room and I had Alvin get ready the car just in case. As a Singaporean, it's probably not very convenient for him to drive his own car if he has to get around, and we might not always be able to get a taxi in a hurry. So if he's going out – who checks into a hotel and stays in all day, don't they have souvenirs to buy? – we had to be ready to tail him.

My guess was correct. An hour after he went up to his room, he came down and was picked up by the same cream-coloured SUV we saw the night before, driven by the same woman. We followed them as they drove to the nearby shopping centre. The wonderful thing about being in a different country, is something kids also experience when they change schools, say, at the end of primary six: in a new place, you can do anything you want, be anyone you want to be, especially when you are posted to a school that many of your classmates didn't pick. Here, our subject must have felt no one knew him too. He and the woman who picked him were holding hands in public as they walked up the overhead bridge, chatting happily and within limits in a conservative Muslim country, they touched each other easily. The easy intimacy was for all to see, and we captured it on camera.

They had a meal and went back to the hotel. I reminded myself again that it was good to have a local resource like Alvin. I would probably have gotten lost driving here and there, but Alvin drove fine and managed to tail them from a safe distance, giving me the chance to run the next steps in my head.

At the hotel, Mr Hock and his companion, a slim-built Chinese lady that looked in her 40s, went up the lift and to his room. How did I know? I was in the lift with them. They were holding hands because they had no idea I was actually following them. I even got out on the same floor they did.

I already knew which room they would go into, so I stopped a few doors short and pretended to fumble for my keys in front of a room that wasn't mine. I dropped the keys too, and leisurely picked them up. Hock and his lady friend were in a much greater hurry. It's not good to be seen too long along the corridor – it's just instinct, I guess, even if you are in a foreign country.

They just swiped the card and slipped right into the room. I waited a while then went over. From the little gap under the door, I could tell the lights were off and the whole room was in darkness, as when even the curtains are drawn. A while later, I also heard a man's groaning from beyond the door. The subject, I presume.

It took them three hours to re-surface at the hotel lobby. This time, the woman drove off on her own. She got what she wanted, so did our subject; and so did we.

# CHAPTER 8

# PROJECT MEMORIES

We get enough assignments from husbands and wives calling upon our services to look into the supposed secret lives of their beloved spouses – whether the latter is, horror of horrors, cheating on them. Well, we also do a fair amount of business with similar requests from suspicious boyfriends and girlfriends, too.

Technically, it isn't adultery if the couple isn't married in the first place. But there are reasonable expectations of exclusivity in a relationship; expectations which are not met when one party is keeping someone else's bed warm without the partner's knowledge. We call it cheating!

We had one such case when a lady walked into our office and asked for her boyfriend to be tailed. She was tall, slim, and quite the stunner in her own understated way; and a good dresser too, though quite subdued.

"I think my boyfriend is cheating on me with a China woman. Is it possible to have him followed? We are not married so would that be a problem?"

"It would be more of a problem for you if you were married. We are a private agency, we are not concerned that you don't have an official relationship with this person; to us, it is an assignment, and we would be happy to take it on if the terms are right."

Of course I had to explain to Miss Wang, my prospective client, that we do not guarantee results and we will not do anything that will compromise the safety of the public and our investigators. Having accepted our terms and charges, Miss Wang supplied us with a physical description of her boyfriend, the make, colour and registration number of his car, and naturally, his home and office address. She also supplied us with an image of an e-ticket bearing her boyfriend's name for an upcoming trip to China, dated one month from the day we met. All that was left then, was for us to follow him about, see what Prince Charming's been up to.

Miss Wang informed us that her boyfriend, Derek, was working late that night, so I went down to his office. When I'm working on my own, I prefer to ride a bike. It saves fuel, I can park anywhere, and if the subject is driving, it's not very likely that he will notice he's being followed, since to most drivers, motorcyclists are faceless and everyone looks the same... unless you have a very nice bike with a stand-out sound, which of course I don't.

It was a little before 10 pm and the industrial estate where Derek's office was located was already quite deserted so I spotted the black Mazda 6 easily. So our subject (Derek) was indeed hard at work, there was no reason to doubt this. Yet. I made myself comfortable and waited from a discreet distance that allowed me to keep watch on the subject's car.

Some 45 minutes later, I saw the subject – fitting my client's description of a large-built Chinese man with tanned complexion and short hair – walking out of the building and get into the car I was observing. I tailed him on my bike to Ang Mo Kio. I thought he would be headed home, but he drove to another part of Ang Mo Kio and picked up a Chinese man. They then continued on their way, and eventually we ended up at Memories Music Lounge.

This was going to be a long night. I looked at my watch as the two men made their way into the lounge: it was 11 pm. If it was one of the larger KTVs, I would have followed them into the establishment; got myself a drink and wait in air-conditioned comfort for the subject and his kaki to finish their business. But this was only a small late-night joint, located in a two-storey shophouse. There would be no place for me to observe them without being noticed. So I waited outside.

What happens at a late night music lounge? Nothing on the outside, all the fun is indoors. At regular intervals, patrons or some of the working girls in there would come out for a short while. Not to smoke; they can do that inside, but to answer phone calls. Open door, blast of music, someone comes out. Then another door, with another blast of music, and they go in. I was bored to tears and the mosquitoes were having a better time. But that's just part of the job.

It wasn't till almost 4 am that my subject surfaced, and he wasn't alone: he was accompanied by a lady in her 20s, slim, very pretty and from all the sequins and shiny bits she had on her dark coloured dress, obviously a working girl at the music lounge. I quickly noted her physical characteristics: it was too dark to take a photo and who knows this woman might surface again in our surveillance.

They got into the subject's car, and he drove to Balestier, where she alighted and went into one of the apartments in a low-rise block. The subject then drove to Ang Mo Kio where he stays, and went up to his apartment. It was 4:15 am. I waited for another half an hour and decided to leave when there were no more movements from our very busy subject.

A couple of days later, we were tipped off by our client that her boyfriend was seeing a client at 5 pm. Well, acting on a hunch, we made our way to Balestier, where I had seen the subject drop off the woman from the music lounge. True enough, we found his black Mazda 6 parked along the road. What client might our subject be seeing here, seeing that he worked in the chemicals industry?

I waited for around half an hour before I saw the subject leave the second-floor apartment where the woman had entered the previous night. He was accompanied by a different woman. This woman with him was older, in her 30s. Both of them walked briskly to the subject's car and seemed to be waiting for someone. The woman who looked to be in her 30s was dressed in a black blouse with three-quarter pants and took the backseat.

A few minutes later, the woman I saw the other night appeared, dressed in simpler clothes: a blue blouse and a white printed skirt. She took the front seat, and the three of them drove off. To where, I wondered? A rather odd work meeting.

The subject drove to the area where Memories Music Lounge was located. And there, all three trooped into a steamboat restaurant a few streets away. Through the large glass windows, I could see that they were having their dinner. The subject also held the younger woman's hand during the meal. That's enough reason to believe then that our subject had a regular relationship with this woman, I made a note to label her as "co-subject" in my reports.

After the meal, the subject drove the two women to the nearby music lounge. Here, the older woman alighted first and went into the lounge, while the younger woman lingered in the car with the subject. I couldn't quite see through the glass from where I was standing; the younger woman – the co-subject – soon alighted and walked into music lounge while the subject drove off. I tailed him to his home before I ceased the day's surveillance. The subject had a meeting with a client in a sense. I was getting more convinced he was the client in the meeting.

Guys who frequent the music lounge or KTV circuit generally get to know a regular girl before too long. It's like a friendship association. Over drinks, song and dance, casual relationships are made. Girls come and go in the business. Their patrons could also tire of the usual fare and easily move on to new linkages. In the case for our subject, having steamboat elevates the standing of the relationship into something more regular, I suppose. Perhaps nothing much, but there was certainly something stirring between those two.

A week passed before we set out to observe our subject again. It was a week day, and we were informed by our client that her boyfriend would be back very late. He had a meeting and after that had to entertain a client who was just in town. We expected this was another ruse to see the co-subject from the music lounge.

Just a few days before, a handful of us at the office – a lone operator would likely attract more attention – had gone down to Memories Music Lounge to check out the place. Nice cosy place; the only chance of observing it up close was to go in as paying customers. We felt it was necessary to understand a little more about the background and context of the relationship we were investigating.

It didn't take long to spot our co-subject. She was one of the singers on stage! We had a few drinks and sang a few songs for the sake of putting up a convincing front as stressed-out office workers. We left without drawing too much attention; but not before exchanging phone numbers... you never know when you might need the contacts for other cases.

Well, on this Tuesday afternoon, the subject was supposed to entertain some overseas clients from out of town. But it was more likely a chance to meet his lady friend – not our client. Our hunch was right. Having planted ourselves outside the Balestier apartment that the co-subject stayed in, our subject duly arrived in his car a little before 5 pm.

We saw him knock on the ground floor door and spoke to someone on his mobile phone. Moments later, a bunch of keys were thrown from the second floor window. The subject picked them up and used them to let himself into the apartment. It was an amusing scene, really. Our subject stayed in the apartment for a good two hours. My tea got cold but what could I do.

Our lovebirds appeared briefly two hours later, on the balcony. Wearing a flimsy looking yellow T-shirt and running shorts, the co-subject was bringing in her laundry while the subject looked on; they were chatting and laughing. They went in and reappeared 10 minutes later, making their way to the car. I was ready for them, of course. We can't just react, we have to anticipate; and that comes with experience.

They drove to the same steamboat restaurant for dinner, before making their way to the music lounge. And there, in the parking lot, I saw the two kissing in the car. It was dark; but the moonlight was bright enough. After that, she went to work, he went home.

This would become something like a routine. The subject would pick up the co-subject for dinner, then send her to work at the music lounge. Sometimes they would meet in the afternoon before that. One Saturday morning we found the subject's black Mazda 6 parked on the back lot of a budget hotel near the co-subject's home. During the course of our surveliance, there was enough hand-holding over dinner and kissing in the car park that we captured on camera.

On the day of the flight according to the e-ticket that our client supplied us, we also confirmed that our subject was flying off to China together with the co-subject: we photographed them checking in together on the day of the trip.

Well then, as I told my client the first day we met; it would have been a problem if my client and the subject were married.

CHAPTER 9

# INTERNATIONAL SIN CITY

I have said before that to cheat is something very primary to our self-serving nature. Maybe it's to survive when we were apes, as some say. To survive, to get an advantage here and more leverage there which hopefully adds up to a difference in fortunes, be it life or death, success or failure. And even as we are bit hesitant to break the law – commercial fraud could land one in jail, and people entering a thought about shop lifting have to contend with the scary posters displayed at the shop front – the barrier to personal betrayals seem somewhat lower. People will cheat on their spouse!

So it's not really a misconception that many of our cases involve wives checking on their husbands and vice versa. Though we can pretty much find out anything that an Internet browser can reveal to you, we find ourselves tailing errant wives and husbands, much of the time. And this has ballooned in recent years.

You can blame the media if you want. It looks to me the most instant evil in corrupting our society, youth and grown-ups alike. We hear enough complaints about the young become more self-centred and materialistic as a result to watching too much TV or spending too much time online. Well, it seems to me it's all the same. If we are awash in an alien set of values courtesy of mass media, then all groups are similarly exposed and... decomposing! I don't think the young are very much more impressionable than older adults, and they are also closing the gap in terms of worldliness. Along the same logic, married couples, spending more of their waking life apart and at work, just have more opportunity to live out the message of permissiveness that we blame the media for spreading.

As a country, we have also become a hub of many sorts. As a port in the past, we were a gateway. People and businesses come here as a springboard to elsewhere in the region, as far north as China, as one of our leaders famously touted our "guan xi" to a rapt international audience. But we have grown from a springboard into a hub, the world now comes to Singapore!

At one time, we were tracking multiple husbands playing the field with multiple nationalities: a middle-aged office manager who had the seniority to sneak off during lunch for trysts with a Filipino barmaid at short-time budget hotels, before sending her to work in his black Mercedes; a restaurant supervisor with a thing for his Vietnamese colleague; an IT project manager working around Chinatown who enjoyed stolen intimacies with a Chinese nurse working at nearby Singapore General Hospital; and we even tracked one subject all the way to Shenzhen when he flew over on a "business trip". When it comes to adultery, every major age, income group, race and nationality is covered.

"We've been married for more than 20 years!" Mrs Lim had begun to take a greater interest in her husband's activities as they grew apart, what with their two children being more independent and spending more time at school, and there supposedly was less to do other than look at each other. Yet, instead of work activities tapering off with age and seniority (the hectic, all-consuming career building phase should in theory be over for them, since they were now in their 50s), instead of having tea at the community centre or walks by the beach and other nostalgic attractions in Singapore and abroad, she was seeing less and less of her husband, who seemed as busy as ever.

"I called the office one afternoon to ask if he was coming back for dinner and you know what? His staff said he was not around, not yet back from lunch. At 4 o'clock in the afternoon? They told me sometimes there isn't much to do right now as they had just completed a major project and it's not a peak season for them. So why is he still working so late, night after night? And I was told he goes out quite often, but he's the manager, and so far there has been no problems so no one's made a fuss. But there is a problem for us. I don't know what he does. And even after he's home, he goes out and stays out late also. Even our kids don't do that! So I want you to look into this. Tell me what he's been doing."

For the next three nights, we tailed Mr Lim after work. On the first night, he came home at 8 pm and left again within half an hour, even though it was raining heavily. We lost track of him after he beat the lights at a junction. I didn't think it was because he knew he was being followed, he just happened to drive pretty recklessly. We found him beating the lights on a few occasions even within the eight-day period that we had agreed upon with his wife to put him under surveillance. Who says senior folk drive slow? I suppose how one drives is a force of habit.

One night – a public holiday, no work – we took a chance that he wasn't going to stay home and watch the holiday specials on TV with his wife, so we staked out his condo from the afternoon around 5 pm. True enough, we saw Mr Lim leaving the house at 5:15 pm and drive off on his own. We followed him to a Catholic church. Makes sense as it was Christmas Day. He stayed in the church for around an hour and after that, we tailed him driving aimlessly about town, till he went for dinner, then ended the night at a pub.

On day four, we got something when we changed tack to monitor his lunch hours. At around 12:30 pm (lunch hour), we saw Mr Lim going towards his car and drive off. We followed him to a housing estate, and we had to keep a distance as he parked along the side of the road and sat waiting in the car. For around 20 minutes, our subject kept the engine running the whole time. Then we saw a Filipino woman in her 30s, with shoulder length hair and wearing an orange top and white shorts, hop into the car and the subject quickly drove off. While travelling along Lavender Road, our subject beat the lights again and we lost him. Here, having a hunch was important. Where could our subject go in this area? Lavender is a budget hotel area after all, so the options can be narrowed down a fair bit. We rode around the area and true enough, found his car on the backlot of one of the budget hotels in the area.

We waited around an hour and a half – it doesn't take long to finish the deed and budget hotels charge room rates in lots of two hours – and saw Mr Lim and the Filipino woman walking towards the car at around 3 pm. I guess you can say they were discreet; they weren't holding hands. Our subject dropped off the Filipino woman along Merchant Road – I made a mental note that there was a row of pubs there, so presumably her place of work was among one of these. Then Mr Lim drove back to his office, reaching it at 3:30 pm – a long lunch.

We were going to tail Mr Lim the whole day, so we waited at the car park where we could keep an eye on his car. Promptly at 6:30 pm, Mr Lim strode into the car park. What happened to doing overtime? Well. He reached home before 7 pm, and stayed there till 10 pm. He had changed into something more casual from the usual work attire (long sleeved shirt and pants for managers), and was in a striped polo T-shirt and dark coloured pants. We tailed his vehicle to the Merchant Road area, where he parked and walked a short distance on foot into one of the pubs in the area called Happy Hands (name of the pub changed, obviously).

Happy Hands is quite typical of the many Filipino pubs that have sprouted all over Singapore. These pubs gained notoriety at Tanjong Pagar because a Member of Parliament expressed his shock at the brazenness of their activity in public view. And after many police sweeps, they have largely vacated that area to find new homes in other locales.

I personally find these pubs a waste of money. The atmosphere is cheerful enough and can be suitably rowdy. After a day's work, it's not bad to relax over some beers, enjoy the music and have some company. But it can get prohibitively expensive buying the ladies drinks at $10, $20 or $50 a pop, just so one doesn't appear cheap. I mean, if you just want to drink, you could have that at the coffee shop. But with female company, some conversation, and the occasional grope, a Filipino bar it is; it just costs a lot.

Not only did I follow Mr Lim into the pub, I also established that the Filipino woman he checked into the hotel with that afternoon, was working at the pub. "Who's that lady in the cream dress?" I asked Linda, the girl who had shown me to my table and already hooked her arm around mine. As a matter of course, I also bought her a ladies drink, to keep up appearances and get some information. "So naughty! I'm your girlfriend tonight!" After some pretend protests, the girl let on that the woman's name was Maria. "No, I just thought she looked familiar. Of course it's only you I'm drinking with tonight." Mr Lim was actually sitting alone, while Maria was busy entertaining other guests. I made a little more aimless small talk with Linda and made my excuses to leave before it came time to buy her another round of drinks. I left the pub and waited outside for Mr Lim.

I don't know how he keeps it up at his age. Mr Lim must have gotten impatient. He left the pub in about an hour, at around half past 12, and instead of heading home, I followed him to Orchard Towers, where he sat drinking till past 2 am before heading home.

Over the next few days, Mr Lim made a habit of meeting Maria for lunch, beating the traffic lights, and checking into a hotel in the Lavender area before sending the latter to work at Happy Hands. Always the same woman, we managed to compile quite a portfolio of photos of them together at lunch, over coffee, all that fetching to and fro while he was supposed to be at work. And on a subsequent visit to Happy Hands, we also made direct contact with Maria herself. Getting her mobile phone number was as simple as just asking for it, and we did that to ascertain her identity.

What can I say? Another victim of globalisation.

CHAPTER 11

# A SURPRISING TWIST

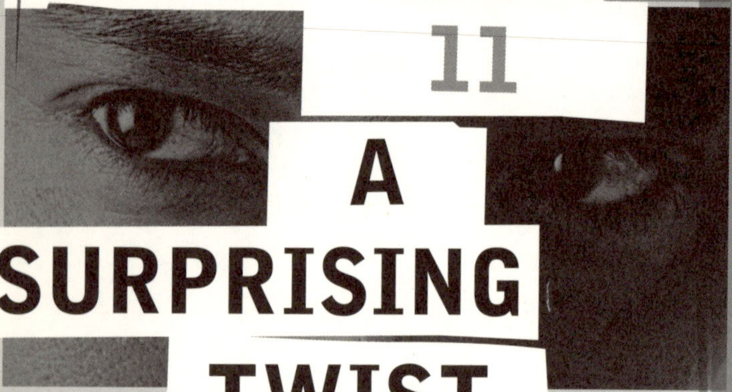

I suppose by now you think that a lot of the cases that a private investigator handles are extra maritial affairs or what we term as EMAs. Well while EMAs do constitute a fair bit of business, no two cases are alike. Even seasoned old hands like us do encounter twists when investigating what appears to be a routine cheating spouse case.

Mrs Ong called and made an appointment to see us. "Mr Heng, you came highly recommended. Your company helped my friend gather evidence that her husband was having an affair with his secretary. I want to engage your services."

We get many of our cases by word of mouth or recommendations. Just like a renovation contractor, if you do a good job, your client is likely to recommend you to her friends and relatives. We do pride ourselves on our excellent success rate and are known to be very discreet.

Back to the case at hand. Mrs Ong looked to be in her early 30s. She was dressed in a branded designer suit with matching handbag and shoes and looked every bit the successful career woman she was. She sat down and took off her large sunglases.

"I believe my husband is having an affair. We are both busy with our careers and I do spend a few days every month on overseas business trips. Although his behaviour towards me has not changed, I sense a difference in his attitude.

"Recently I noticed that my husband has been receiving text messages on his mobile phone late at night and secretly smiling to himself.

"He takes more pride in his appearance and has started using the gym at our condominium on a daily basis. What's more, he has bought a lot of new clothes including expensive designer underwear."

I explained our fee structure and mode of operations and reminded Mrs Ong that the results of our investigation may not always be the result the client is expecting.

Without batting an eyelid, she took out her cheque book and wrote us a cheque covering a week's work. She would be away in ten days time and suggested that it would be a good time to watch her husband. Mrs Ong also supplied a photograph of her husband and provided details of his car, his workplace and a list of places he was known to visit in his leisure hours. She was definitely organised.

Before leaving, she said, "I win at everything I do. I will not lose to another woman. I expect a full report when I am back from my business trip."

Mr John Ong headed the finance department in a local SME. From what we checked, his job was desk bound so it appeared to be a piece of cake to shadow him. I drew up a schedule and briefed the team who were to work on his case.

On the first day of surveillance, my colleague Chandran waited on his motorcycle outside the main entrance of the condominium where the Ongs were staying. When Mr Ong left at 8 am, Chandran quietly followed the black BMW until they reach the factory building in Kallang where Mr Ong worked.

There was a food centre opposite the factory. Chandran settled down and ordered some food. It would be a long wait. He could see Mr Ong's car and the main entrance to the building. So even if the suspect were to leave in another vehicle, we could still trail him. Other than a quick lunch at the food centre, Mr Ong remained at work the whole day.

After work, Mr Ong drove to Marina Square where he met another gentleman for dinner. Chandran was able to observe them as they took a table beside the window. It looked like any business meeting, they shook hands and ordered, chatting earnestly throughout the meal. After dinner, Mr Ong drove home and Chandran monitored the apartment from across the road. When the lights went out at midnight and Mr Ong did not appear after 30 minutes, it was time to call it a day.

We repeated this same routine on the next two days.

Mr Ong met different men for dinner but they looked very professional and there was definitely no other woman. If he was having an affair he was being very discreet.

On day four of the case, there appeared to be some developments. Mr Ong normally left the office at 6:45 pm but today, he suddenly came out of his office at 5 pm and walked towards his car. George who was assigned to shadow our suspect quickly got on his motorcycle, reported his status to HQ and waited.

Mr Ong drove to New Bridge Road and parked at the multi-storey car park at Chinatown Complex. He had a bowl of bean curd at the food centre and kept looking at his watch. He appeared to be waiting.

"Beep Beep." He received a text message on his phone. He finished his dessert and quickly walked towards the shophouses in one of the lanes nearby where he entered a doorway.

George quickened his footsteps and came to a frosted glass door. It said "SPA For men only". He entered and approached the small reception area. George paid the fee and signed the guestbook with his real name and NRIC number below all the other illegible squiggles. This was important as PIs are sometimes called as witnesses in trials and other cases and needed to establish their presence in any particular place.

The receptionist who looked like a poly student gave him a towel, a short cotton robe and pressed the buzzer to open the door leading to the spa. George went in and found himself in a locker area. Ah! The subject was in the corner changing out of his office attire.

Opening the locker, George saw a condom and it dawned on him that this was possibly one of the gay establishments he had heard about. But there was no time to think and ponder as the subject was already closing his locker. George quickly changed and wrapping his towel around him headed out of the locker room.

As his eyes adjusted to the dim lighting, George saw Mr Ong sitting on a sofa chatting with another man. He just stood nearby and leaned against the wall. While this act may seem conspicious in any other situation, it was common in a gay spa to stand around and wait to catch the attention of someone you fancied. Some of the other patrons tried to smile and make eye contact with George but the scowl on his face deterred them from approaching him or try to initiate a conversation.

Soon Mr Ong and his friend walked down a dark corridor where there were a number of rooms and disappeared into one of them. George peeped into an empty room and saw a PVC-covered mattress and a basket filled with used tissue. George waited outside the room Mr Ong had entered. Through the paper thin walls, he could hear what was happening inside. Although he felt rather nauseated, this was work and he had to do his job. After 45 minutes, the couple left the room, showered and got dressed.

George followed them to the Chinatown food centre. He quickly sat at the next table where he could eavesdrop on what they were saying. They sat opposite each other and were bitching about work and while it appeared innocent to the bystander, the trained eye noticed that they were sharing a large glass of sugarcane juice and using one straw. They were definitely more than casual friends. On the pretext of sending an SMS, George took some photos of them using his mobile phone.

When my client returned from her business trip, the report was ready for her. As I said earlier, the results of our investigation are not always what the client expect. In this instance, while Mrs Ong was still the number one woman in her husband's life, it was a blow to discover that he was bisexual and also enjoyed having sex with men.

# CHAPTER 10

# A DIFFERENT BREED

Just what kind of people will thrive as private investigators? That is not that difficult to answer; living it is much trickier. Put simply, a little of everything. Unlike most professions where the environment is relatively static, the competent PI has to be very adaptable, able to be comfortable in any situation in order to do the appropriate thing to maintain his cover and still be resourceful enough to get his job done.

Perhaps you will think that in teaching, the learning environment is always dynamic. Or that situations change from minute to minute for people who work as stock brokers. These jobs can hardly be described as "static" in a sense. But the nature of each job remains the same, even if it changes – within pretty well-defined limits.

A private investigator is a whole different scale of dynamic when you consider that in seeking out the truth about all kinds of people and situations, we have to play many parts, inhabit many environments, to get within reach of answers. Some private investigators love to show off a roomful of special equipment: microphones that can capture conversations from a few tables away, cameras that fit into a bewildering array of innocent everyday objects, skeleton keys that pick numerous locks. Even the mobile phone these days can do so much, it's no longer just a humble little device for making calls, we can use it to shoot stills, capture video, record audio, even GPS should we get lost.

But the most important tools aren't these gadgets. It's no cliché, the most important resource in a private investigator's arsenal is the brain; our wits. We could be tailing someone at the golf course, at the teahouse, in a bus; we could even take up bogus posts in a company to keep tabs on certain employees. And in all these assignments, like good actors, we have to look the part. There are no re-takes. We've got to play golf like we know how, make tea like we could be doing it all day, ride a bus and keep our subject under observation without looking any different from the hundreds of thousands of faceless commuters that use the transport system each day.

We've got to dabble in everything, to have an interest in everything, and we have to think on our feet. And of course, we also need to have a web of contacts. Contacts built on goodwill, cemented by mutual self-interest. When a subject steps into a hotel, chances are, we already know the people at the counter, who can give us pointers, or at least not be overly obstructive as we track our subject. And we also work with the police, now and then. Why? Because often enough, our cases overlap. And when we come across criminal offences we would work together with the police.

Is this line of work dangerous? It certainly could be. Sometimes what we investigate can put a lot at stake for the people being investigated. Just adultery cases alone, we are talking personal reputations, breakups of families, division of assets and even custody of children. Would people hurt others with such things in the balance? Certainly, we've all known people to turn nasty over much less.

But at the end of the day, though the nature of the job might be quite different from those mentioned by virtue of its dynamism, the very same thing lies at the heart of what motivates people to be good at what they do: passion. You've got to have a certain passion for the job, even if it might not be easy to admit it, because saying you're passionate about work that is hard to do makes one look a little stupid, like a sucker for tough love. But the passion is there; it's got to be. That's why I do it.

# APPENDIX

# HOW TO KNOW YOUR SPOUSE IS CHEATING

Adultery is not just an act, it is a state of mind; and as such it leaves clues in body language and behaviour that can be deciphered if you know how to read the signs. But there is something to note: books are hard enough to read that you can get a GCE paper for doing it right; in comparison, people can be a little more complex and the signs, conflicting. So you can bear the following markers in mind, but you still have to measure what you observe against what you know of your spouse in order to make a judgement on whether to give us a call!

## CHARM OFFENSIVE

When your wife or husband is being extra nice all of a sudden, it could be a guilt thing that they are trying to get over. Flowers for no reason? A handbag? A watch? Usually it's a gift of an object, rather than time, like a dinner, a date, etc. Because the object/present is supposed to scrub one's conscience clean and also take the place of honest intimacy that is hard to achieve when bearing a cheating heart and mind. If your spouse has been buying you presents every now and then anyway, then it could be nothing; perhaps the husband feels sorry that he's spending too much time at work, and the only sure, tangible way to reach you is with something nice bought at retail; perhaps the wife just feels like buying something for you. Pay attention to signs but don't get overly concerned with them, people cannot be read like instruments used in a lab.

## TIME APART

Overtime again? Hanging out with friends again? Well work is rightly demanding if we have to keep up our importance as a GDP superstar. But how much time can a person spend at work before the home unravels? Is your husband or wife really that busy? Or has your spouse passed some point in the sand where work becomes a welcome, justified outlet to spend time away from family? When that line is crossed, temptation and adultery is not slow to follow.

## TIME TOGETHER

Is something different in the air when you're together lately? Is there like an openness from before that is now oddly missing? When you're together, do you touch hands less, or less spontaneously, or the eyes don't really meet? It may not be that your spouse is actually seeing someone else. It could actually be something at work. And you really have to judge based on what was the norm before. That said, when the eyes don't meet, it is usually something personal that involves you, rather than some external issue that has been troubling or distracting your spouse of late.

## THE PHONE

No man is an island, and this is doubly true when everyone's packing a mobile phone. You can think of the phone as a game machine, Facebook on the go or whatever, but where we are concerned, it's actually a magic doorway to relationships that is yet small enough to pocket or bring to the bathroom. Phone calls at odd hours is no longer very strange in our sleepless city, but the fuss over stepping away to answer the call is some cause for concern, while the speaking tone used is a dead giveaway. We just naturally speak differently to different people depending on the nature of the relationship. Voice calls are one thing, text messaging is a whole more discreet kettle of fish. And there is very little one cannot do with mere words. It's not nice to look into your spouse's phone. But seeing how he or she uses it, is an important clue.

## A SHORTER FUSE

I know we said earlier that a guilty conscience makes a cheating husband or wife extra nice to even out the guilt. It could also make them more short tempered, very irritable and always finding fault with you. Why? Because it is also a part of guilt management: if the cheating spouse is always consciously and subconsciously finding fault with their partner over the littlest matter... it could be they are finding that elusive justification to cheat: makes it a little easier on the conscience to cheat against a spouse that is far from perfect.

## SELF IMPROVEMENT

And speaking of perfection, I would take notice too, if your spouse suddenly starts to pay more attention to physical, outward appearance. Who are concerned over looking good, smelling great and dressing well? Dating people. If a husband starts getting very concerned about his lovehandles, or the wife starts to dress a little out of character, it doesn't always mean they are cheating. But for sure, something is changing, or evolving in their frame of mind. Start communicating, find out what's going on, don't just sit still and wait for the emotional distance can grow. When that happens, you might find yourself giving us a call.

## PASSPORT CONTROL

It's amazing these days that we can just hop onto a plane with no fuss at all; it's like taking a bus, just longer distance, and the whole of Asia is one's playground. A part of vigilance includes occasional browsing of the spouse's passport. If the immigration stamp on the page doesn't agree with what you been told, it's a red flag!

# ABOUT THE AUTHOR

A former investigator with the Singapore Police Force, Heng Ping Kai runs Infinity Investigations Pte Ltd, one of the most successful private investigation agencies in the country. Heng and his team have handled a very broad range of cases all over Southeast Asia, from investigating errant spouses, business partners, to finding information about persons and companies, and have also been consulted on security arrangements for MNCs.

Infinity Investigations can be reached at 9710 9719 or via email at heng@infinity-investigations.com